C000061469

READ HINDI IN
20 DAYS

COMPILED BY
SATASH SINGH

WWW.CARIBBEANTRAKKER.COM

PREFACE

Welcome to Read Hindi in 20 days! To begin I would like to say that like you I also wanted to grasp a different language and for many years, I have tried to Read the Hindi language. Many us believe that if we can write a specific language we can also read, speak and understand it. But this is far from the truth.

The four methods of writing, reading, speaking and understanding a language is what is needed to really say you know a language. All the senses help with this development of language just like a child. For example, to speak to someone you must be able to think, and to understand what someone is saying, you must comprehend. But just because you can read a language does not mean that you can write it, and the same way is for understanding a language it does not mean that you can speak it. Over the past few years I have tried to learn other languages like French and Spanish. I learned very fast to read them long before I could write them. For the matter of fact, I could read these languages fairly well before I could speak them.

Hindi is a challenging language to people who speak the English language, because of the construction of the Hindi sentences. The verb is in the end of Hindi sentence while in the English language it is in the middle of the sentence. This causes understanding the Hindi language to be confusing. For example, "nazdeek telefon kahan hai?" when translated is exactly to English is "near telephone where is?" but it means 'where is the nearest phone'.

As a pupil of the Hindi language I even tried taking Hindi classes to learn the language. After a while, I figured that I should research the language using all avenues open to me, including the web. I wanted to understand the Hindi songs that I listen to all the time, but never quite understood it.

This book is a direct compilation of my research. Let me say this, I do not profess to knowing the Hindi language, and sometimes I even worry that I even know the English language. I also do not make any representation that I can write, read, or speak Hindi; as I am still a learner of all these faculties.

I do hope that this book is of help to you if you are learning Hindi, as it is a beautiful language as a difficult one. Please feel free to send me any remarks good, bad and maybe indifferent.

I wish you the best of luck on your journey of learning.

Satash Singh

Table of Contents

DAY 1

Letters S, N , M , K and R This is the Hindi letter S as in Surf

स S

and this is the letter N as in NuN.

ण N

If we join them together we get the word, can you guess what it might be?

सन SN (SUN)

Yes it is Sun!!

Let us look at some more letters.
This is the letter K as in stuck. Note all Hindi letters have a line on top and only the short sound is pronounced.

क K

The next two letters are M and N.

म M

M as in MuM

न N

N as in NuN

To make a word we just join the letters together again so that the top line becomes continuous for e.g. mn (mind)

मन

Now look at these four letters again

स S   क K

म M   न N

Sit back visualize these in your mind and say them aloud.

स S, क K, म M and न N

Now for a real tough test to see if you can read your first word in Hindi

नमक

(nmk--pronounced as namuk -salt)

If you got it right -well done. Award yourself a golden point. Now learn another letter making the R sound as in Rum.

र

Lets read another word - to do –

kr - कर.

Remember the five letters we have learnt

S स K क M म N न and R र.

Visualize all five again

स S, क K, म M, न N and R र

What's this word -die –

मर

.. yes it mr (murr).

and this one?

रम   rm (Rum)

and this is रन   rn (Run)

Now see if you can read your first sentence in Hindi

नमक कम कर

Nmk   km   kr
(namak kam kar)
namak – salt
kam – less
kar – do

salt less do i.e. make it less salty!

Well done.

This is a test to see if you can match the following words Sir, Run , Rum , Rusk , Musk. You get one point for each correct answer.

रसक   रन   सर   मसक   रम

Answers Rusk, Run, Sir, Musk and Rum

Let me remind you that in the words in this Day e.g. in Musk the letter S is only half pronounced and should be written in its half form.

ऱ्

half S

So the word Musk above really reads as Masak. To write it phonetically we should use the half S as below.

मस्क

m half S K

One can get too carried away about half letters and some Indian languages like Punjabi don't have them. If in doubt don't use it. You have come to the end of Day 1.

For an easy end to this Day guess what these numbers are in Hindi . They are being used less and less being replaced by our common English numbers 1, 2, 3 etc.

० १ २ ३ ४ ५ ६ ७ ८ ९

Go over the Day again and again.
Write out the English letters as below and fill in the blanks as you go through the Days. The five letters K M N R and S and half letter S are done for you. Keep referring to this figure as you go through the Days.

Letters and half letters

A B C D E F G H

I J Kख **L M**म **N**न **O P**

Q Rर Sस रT U V W X

Y Z SH Ns Rs

Chest Sounds

KH GH CH CHH JH SHH

Ts

TTH DH AD ADH

Soft Ts

T TH THE THHE

Compound

KSH TR GY RI

LRI OM

Vowels and vowel marks

A AA I EE U OO

AE AAE O OU

In the next lesson I will introduce the vowels

DAY 2

Alphabet small size

Detached vowels

a	aa	i	ee	u	oo	ri

अ आ इ ई उ ऊ ऋ   ae

aae	o	au	an	ah

ए ऐ ओ औ अं अः

Vowel signs

aa	i	ee	u	oo	ae	aae	o

ा ि ी ु ू ॅ ॆ ो

au	ri

ौ ृ

gutturals from the back of your throat

k	kh	g	gh	n

क ख ग घ ङ

palatals touch your tongue to the hard upper palate

ch   chh   j   jh   n

च छ ज झ ञ

cerebrals roll your tongue right back

t   tth   da dh   n

ट ठ ड ढ ण

Dentals touch your tongue to your teeth.

t'   th' th   thh   n

त थ द ध न

labials say with your lips closed

p   f   b   bh   m

प फ ब भ म

semi vowels say it with your lips and throat open

y   r   l   v   sh   shh   s   h

य र ल व श ष स ह

compound and others

ksh	tr	gy	shr	z	ud	udh
क्ष	त्र	ज्ञ	श्र	ज़	ड़	ढ़

t't'	tt	tthtth	theththe	they	n
त	द्द	द्दु	द्ध	द्य	रा

half g	half k
क्	ह्

Check to see if you can remember them

अ आ इ ई उ ऊ ऋ

ए ऐ ओ औ अं अः

क ख ग घ ङ

च छ ज झ ञ

ट ठ ड ढ ण

त थ द ध न

प फ ब भ म

य र ल व श ष स ह

क्ष त्र ज्ञ श्र ज़ ड़ ढ़

त ट ड ढ घ रा क छ

DAY 3

Go over the letters in the last Day. This lesson I am introducing two more constants. This one is Ch as in Church.

च

and the next one S as in Snake स

so for example this word reads as सन **sn (sun)**

and this one is chr (to graze) चर

Next lets take a look at a vowel. A vertical line ा. AFTER a letter makes a long aa sound so

m म becomes मा ...or Maa (mother).

---

see if you can read this word मामा

.... Yes its Maamaa – your mother's brother.

What are the following English words?

मराच   **March ;**

and this one-can you guess what the new letter sounds like?

समारट **Smart!**

Notice the last letter is the T sound. The spelling is strictly not correct as the s should be a half sound but we will deal with that later.

See if you can read following sentence.

राम मारामार न कर सरम कर

ram   maramar   n   kr   saram   kr
You should have read Ram maramar n kr, saram kr - Ram fight don't do, shame be!

For now just go over the one vowel aa sound .... T and the 7 consonants learned ..

क k म m न n र r च ch स s and ट t

To recap what you have learnt so far.

One vowel aa sound .... Ⅰ and 7 consonants ..

क k म m न n र r च ch स s and ट t

As a test see if you can read the word for tomato in Hindi

टमाटर **yes - tmaatr.**

How about truth?

सच **-sch -pronounces as such.**

What's this English word?

कार **Car.**

Let us look at two vowels. The little i or e...

ि

is place in FRONT but pronounced AFTER the letter e.g. this, word below reads Miss as in English.

मिस the line at the top should be joined but overlook that quirk for the moment.

The big ee ी

is placed AFTER the letter. For eg this is the English word Team.

टीम

The following sentence in English has three new letters -for the P sound as in Pup, the L as in Look and the THE sound as in moTHEr.

P प   L ल   THE द

See if you can read this sentence. Remember to fill in your worksheet from Day 1

द टीचर मीतस द पीपल.

The teacher meets the people.
Well done if you got all three correct!

द   pronounce as **THE - soft d; the**

प **p sound as in Purse.**

and the ल **L as in Learn?**

What are the following English words?

द मिनारट सपीक लीच...

Answers - the Minaret; Speak; Leach

Notice that the above three words contain all the ten consonants ----

K L M N P R S T, CH, THE and the vowels AA, Little E and Big EEE learnt so far. Make sure you can recognize them before moving on

DAY 4

This lesson you will learn four more letters -the b sound as in Burn, sh sound as in SHirt, j sound as in Junk, and the z sound as in scarS or maiZe

ब Burn श SHirt ज Junk and ज़ maiZe

Now for a real tough test. What are these English words?

भरक   Bark

शारक   Shark

जिल   Jill

सटारज़ Stars..Notice the Z is just like a J but with a dot below it.

What is this word?

कलीन ंशीट   Clean Sheet.

रिच जज   rich judge

करीप   Creep

बीच   Beech

Next we look at two more vowels.

The little u ु after a letter gives it a short u sound e.g. lOOk

and the big u ू gives it the long ooo as in moon.

When these are put BELOW the letter, it is written as

Look लुक and moon as मून

What's this word?

नून noon ; and this one?

जूस Juice; and this Hindi word

जुलम zulm (injustice).

Now see if you can decode a whole sentence

लालीटा कुकस द चिकन

Lalita cooks the chicken.

If you think this is too easy? Wait until you see the next Day!

DAY 5

Go over the first four Days spending about 5 minutes on each to make sure you have the shape of the letters firmly in your mind.
In this Day, we learn of four more vowels

ॆ **which placed on top of a letter gives it an 'ae' sound as in Ape.**

What is this word?

पेपर **Paper**

A double one on top like this

ॊ **gives it a deeper ae sound as in Apple. What is this word?**

पैरट **Yes Parrot.**

To get the 'O' sound as in Oar we put this after a letter

ो..

What's this word . मोर **its MORE -peacock.**

and finally the deeper 'Au' sound as in crOcodile

ौ

What is this word?

मौली **Molly – a girl's name.**

This is the letter for Y as in Yummy.

य

Can you read this word?

यमयम

That's right - its yumyum..

This is the letter V as in roVer

व

What is this word?

मूव **Move.**

This is H as in Hurt

ह

What is this word?

हट **Answer hut.**

finally, the G sound as in Gum

ग

What is this word?

गन **Gun**

This is a most important sentence in Hindi. Can you read it?

ये कया है

Ye Kyaa Hae? -literally This what is? or what is this? You have now learnt most of the common letters and vowels used in Hindi. if you have come this far the rest is going to be plain sailing. Its important to keep revising each Day.

DAY 6

The vertical line is the aa sound as in faather with the mouth wide open. However there is also a more truncated aa sound with the mouth less open as in the word laaf (laugh) with a little moon shaped sign on top of the vertical line. So the Indians tend to say dactar instead of doctor with the a in dac with the mouth just half open as in the figure below.

डॉक्टर   **dactar**

So when you see the moon over the vertical line remember its only a half aa sound.

The un nasal sound is in two forms.
a) A dot . over the top as in the word rUNg (of a ladder).

रंग

and b) as a longer deeper sound ann

as in the word cANt

कॉट

Two letters which sound similar are the soft t -

त

made with the tip of the tongue touching the back
of the upper top teeth and protruding slightly
beyond them and
the soft th sound with the tongue a bit further back

as in souTH   थ

What's this word?

तोता tota   parrot .

What's this word?

थैंकस   Thanks!

Can you guess what this new letter sounds like

लाफ Laf (laugh) it is the letter F written in

Hindi as

फ

Whats this word?

ट्रैफिक Traffic.

See if you can guess the sound of another letter from this word

मैड maD ie the D is represented by the letter

ड

Whats this word?

जेड Jade.

This is a final test see if you can read this somewhat painful story in English. It has one new letter, see if you can guess the sound.

द बी सटग अमीट

ही टालड हिज़ सीसटोर

शी टोलड हिम नौट टु कराइ

The bee stung John.
He told his sister.
She told him not to cry.

The sound for a vowel i (or little e) is represented
by the letter.

इ.

Note that the L in t-o-l-d should really be a half L
as otherwise the word reads tolud. We will come
to half letters later. Can you identify all the letters
learnt in this Day?
. with un sound as in hung

aan sound as in shant

त   the soft t as when the tongue touches the
bottom teeth -Lata -name of a girl.

थ   the soft th as in mirTH or THud .

फ   The F as in First.

ड   the hard d as in Driver and finally the vowel
sound for little e or i written on its own.

इ   as in drY. Go over the Day again. Next week
we look at more vowels by it self.

DAY 7

Vowels when on their own and not modifying another sound are written differently. The little e was shown in Day 6. Lets look at
A as in Until
Aa as in Army
little e as in Interview
and the big ee as in Easter.
See if you can spot which is which.

अ   A as in Alarm.

आ   Aa as in Artist.

इ   i as in Income and finally

ई   big EE as in craEEm (crime)

What is this sentence in English?

अ मैन आनसरड द डोर

A man answered the door.
and these two?

अकल जैक जौईनड द आरमी

आर यु सीरिअस

Uncle Jack joined the army;
 Are you serious?

आई वान्ट आईस करीम

इन द नाइट

I want ice cream in the night.
Go over the Day again. Notice that v is used in want. There is no letter for w in Hindi and many Indians tend to pronounce w as v. Note also the half n in want. Some people say the n with a nasal sound so you can use a dot instead of the half n.

DAY 8

Detached forms of the Vowels continued

These are the two detached forms of the u

-little u उ and big u ऊ in this sentence.

ड पराउड माऊज़

....The proud mouse!

Little u is उ and big u is ऊ

Similarly, this is the detached form of the vowel ae as in Ape

ए

and the Aae as in mAt.

ऐ

Whats this sentence?

ए ऐरो हिट द एींट

A arrow hit the ant. (OK It was a small arrow).
So little ae is ..

ए   as in Ape

and big aae is

ऐ as in Atomic or @.

O as in Only is written as

ओ

and big au as in autumn as

औ

What is this phrase?

दिस औटम ओनली   This autumn

only.
The letter for o on its own is

ओ and for au on its own is

औ

DAY 9

There are many forms of the letters N. Only the first one displayed is usually used. Some are more nasal than others. It is only important to know about them because you might come across them. Remember only the first one is actually used a lot.

न ङ ण ञ णा

Compound letters
Unlike other Hindi letters, these have two syllables and are probably derived from Sanskrit.

The first is soft t त and r र combined tr त्र

as in Yatra (journey) यात्रा

The next is R and I combined Ri

ऋ as in Rishi (holy man) ऋषि

The next is sh श and r combined shr

श्र **as in Shrap (curse)** श्राप

The next is k. क and sh श combined ksh

क्ष as in क्षत्रिय Kshatriya (warrior)

And finally the G ग and y य gya

ज्ञ as in Gyan (knowledge) ज्ञान

DAY 10

There are some fierce looking letters that are really a combination of two Hindi letters. For example, H and Y combined is hya.

ह्र

They are not used that much but still is important to know them to be able to read Hindi.

Note the second letter is in the foot of the first.
Guess which is the combined form for
D and D (Dd) ;
D and Y (Dya)
D and chesty D (Ddh)
h AND Y (Hya)....Note Y is in foot of H

द्

he-the
raddi – waste

द्य

Thhe-y
Vidhya – knowledge

---

the-thhe
buddha

ह्य

h-y
hya - shame
Although they look difficult, they are just
combining two letters you have already learnt.

Next, try
R and long U (Roo)
L and Ri (Lri)
- Note that the small downward curve is often
used to add a ri sound to many letters. It can be
written at the bottom when it is pronounced after
the letter as in the lri sound here or at the top
when the ri is pronounced before the letter.
and D and V (Dva)

स्व्लृद्ध .

The following round off the combined letters -
two ts, two ths, and two soft ts

इॡत्त.

Do not worry if you find this Day difficult. These letters are rarely used. The only thing left to learn is half letters and numbers and those we will do in the next Day.

DAY 11

Half Letters
Recall the sentence Lalita cooks the chicken

लालीटा कुकस द चिकन

The second word is written here as if pronounced with the full accent on each letter. So it really reads "KOOKUS". To make it as phonetic as possible the second K is written as a half K.
Can you read this?

लालीटा कुक्स

Yes its Lalita cooks, note the second k has been halved.

Nearly all Hindi letters can be written as half letters and the letter is then pronounced with a short clip.
The following images contain sounds for most of the letters. See if you can match each letter to its sound
K, KH, j, soft t, Ksh, Gya, P, N, hard G, Dh, Ch, Chh, B, M, F, Ye, L, Bh. Sh, S, He.

क रव ग ६ फ ा ५

ट छ ज ट र ल ५

& ज ६ ण ८ ९ स ह

The answers going across the top letters of each picture are
K, Kh, hard G, chesty dh, F, M, Bh, F again, M again, Bh again.

The middle letters in each are
Ch, Chh, J, Soft T, Ye, L, V .

and the bottom letters are
Ksh, Gya, B, N, P, Sh, S, H, Ksh again, Gya again, N. There is a chesty Sh which looks like the N above but has a diagonal line.

The following completes the half letters. See if you can guess the sound.

ण ़ ९ ट ट

They are the common N, soft Th, soft T and Ye.

For a real tough test see if you can read this word, it is what you have been learning all along.

हिन्दी

Yes its Hindi! Note the half N.

For an easy end to this Day guess what these numbers are in Hindi. They are being used less and less being replaced by our common numbers 1, 2, 3 etc.

० १ २ ३ ४ ५ ६ ७ ८ ९

Next Day we look at a few more vowel sounds, the letter R and its forms, and after that the complete alphabet.

DAY 12

Letter R

This is a short Day.

The letter R often has the short and long U placed in the middle rather than at the bottom.

What are these words?

रूक   r u k   (rook as in a chess game piece)

रूम   r u m   (room)

A short diagonal stroke also gives an R sound after a letter, usually placed below P or F. Note the R here modifying the first word FAS to what?

फांस

The answer is France! Note the nasal N dot over the F.

A short sign like the one above the letter six on your keyboard is often put under the T give a Tr sound. What is this word?

^ टक ट्रक

Yes, the R modifies the TK to give Truck.

Another is the Ri sound put under M and N but also other letters. What is this word - (Hindi for dance)?

c नृतय

Answer is Nritya.

An R sound can also be placed ABOVE a letter where it is sounded BEFORE the letter it is placed. As a test see if you can read the word below.

मार्क

Many more points if you got the answer right. It is Mark!

DAY 13

Consonants

First Line

These are gutturals produced from the back of the throat.

ख ख ग घ ङ

K   KH   G   GH   N

Gutturals – From the back of your throat

1. K as in hook, Kamra (Room)
2. Kh as in Khaki, Khargosh (rabbit)
3. G as in Gate, Gum (sadness)
4. Gh as in Ghandi, Ghar (house)
5. N

Once again the five letters above are K ; Kh ; G ; Gh ; N

Second Line

These are palatals where the tongue touches the back of the throat.

च छा ज झ ञ

CH CHH J JH N

Palatals – your tongue touches your palate

1. Ch as in Chunkey (tongue touches top of mouth), Chamcha (spoon)
2. Chh as in no equiv in English (tongue touches bottom teeth saying Ch), Chatri (Umbrella)
3. J as in Jungle , Jab (when)
4. Jh as in no equiv in English-tongue touches bottom teeth, in Hindi as in Jhansi , Jhanda(flag)
5. N

The letters are Ch; Chh; J; Jh; N. There is another way of writing JH which is quite popular and we will see that in Day 18

Third Line

These are cerebrals where the tongue is rolled back a bit.

ट ठ ड ढ ण ड़ ढ़

T TTH D DH N ughDh ughDHh

Cerebrals – your tongue rolled all the way back

1. T as in Turkey, tmatur (tomato)

2. Th as in no equiv -tongue curls in more when saying t .....Thandi (cold)

3. D as in Dog, darr (fear)

4. Dh -tongue curls more saying D- no equiv in English, dhakan (lid)

5. N

6. The letter Dh with a dot under it sounds like a combined sound with the tongue curled right back touching the roof and then uncurling hitting the palate and then the back teeth - no equiv in English, in Hindi ladki (girl)

7. ughDH as in paDH (study).

The letters are T, THH , D , DH , N , ughDh and ughDHh

Fourth Line

These are dentals where the tongue touches the teeth

त   थ   द   ध   न

T   TH   THE THHE   N

Dentals – your tongue touches your teeth

1. Soft T (tongue touches top teeth) no

   English equiv, Tabla (drum)
2. Th as in Thanks, haTHi (elephant)
3. Dh as in The, Davat (Invitation)
4. Dhh (from chest -no equiv), Dhanush (Bow)
5. N

The letters are soft T, Th, The, Thh, N

Fifth Line
These are labials where the lips come together.

प   फ   ब   भ   म

P   F   B   BH   M

Labials – keep your lips close together

1. P as in Purse, Patang (Kite)
2. F as in First, Fal (Fruit)
3. B as in Bird, Batakh (Duck)
4. Bh as in no equiv (from chest), Bhalu (Bear)
5. M as in Mum, Matr (Bean)

The above letters are P, F, B, Bh, M.

Sixth Line
These are semivowels

य   र   ल   व

Y   R   L   V

Semi Vowels

1. Y as in Yo, Yug (fire ritual)
2. R as in Run, Rath (Chariot)

3. L as in Lull, Ladhak

4. V as in Vole, Var (Groom)

The above letters are Y, R, L, V.
These are sibilants and the aspirant H

श	ष	स	ह
SH	**SHH**	**S**	**H**

Sibliants
Aspirant

1. Sh as in Shirt, Shalgam (radish)
2. Sh (chesty Sh -no equiv), shatkon (icon).
3. S as in Sup, Sapera (snake charmer)
4. H as in hurt, Hum (us).

The above letters are SH, SHH, S and H

Seventh Line
Next are compound letters.

क्ष	त्र	ज्ञ	श्र	ऋ
KSH (K+SH)	**TR (T+R)**	**GY (G+Y)**	**SHR (SH+R)**	**Ri (R+i)**

Compound Letters

1. Ksh as in no equiv, Kshma (forgive)

2. SoftTr -no equiv -tongue touces top teeth trying to say Tr, Trishul (religious symbol)

3. Ghya no euiv -Ghyan (Knowledge)

4. SHR as in shrug or shrap (curse)

5. Ri as in Wrist or Rishi

The above letters are KSH, TR, GY, SHR and Ri

Next are more compound letters

ध्य   रू   रू   ह्य   ऌ

DY(D+Y)   **RU**   **ROO**   **HY(H+Y)**   **LRi(L+Ri)**

द्ध   द्ध   ङ

DDH   **(D+DH)**   **DV**

Compond Letters

1. Dy as in viDYa -knowledge

2. Ru as in Ruth

3. Roo as in Room

4. HY as in HYundi or HYa (shame)

5. Lri as in Lrissa

6. DDh as in Yuddh (war)

7. DV as in Dwarka (place in India)

8. N'k as in aN'k - letter

9. N'g as in aN'g (limb).

Doubled lettters

त   द्द   ट्ट   ट्ठ   ष्ट

TT(T+T)   **DD(THE+THE)**   **TT**   **TTHTTH**   **SHHT**

ष्ठ   राा

SHHTHH   **N**

Double and other letters

1. tt as in kutta (dog)

2. dd as in saddi –century

3. tt as in lattu (top toy),

4. dd -not shown here as in haddi -bone,

5. tthtth -hatti (stubborn),

6. shht as in nashht (destroy)

7. shhtth

8. N' .

9. Also not written here is Z which is J with a dot underneath it.

Half Letters

Only some are listed below. They are just truncated full letters. As a test, can you guess what they sound like?

क्

Line 1.

ᵈ श् त् र

Line 2.

फ् ᵈ ᵈ

र् ल् ट्

ङ् ज् राा

Line 3.

ख् ग् ठ् स् ट्

ल् श् ट् म्

Line 4.

ठ् म् ट्ट फ

ट ढ़ ऱ ण

ष ऩ

Line 5.
Answers
Line 1 is K .
Figure 2 has n, th, soft t, y
Figure 3 has f, m, bh, y, l, v, ksh, gya, n.
Figure 4 has kh, g, b, s, ch, l, the, j, m.
Figure 5 has b, bh, t (double t), f, gya, ksh, bh, p, gh, m.

Detached Vowels

First Line
1. A as in Umm, Anar (Pomergranate)
2. AA as in Aunt, Aag (Fire)
3. I as in India, Emli (spice)
4. Ee as in East, Eent (brick)
5. U as in oops, ooloo (owl)
6. oo as in moon, oon (yarn).

अ आ इ ई उ ऊ

The vowels are ugh, Aa, i, ee, u and oo

Second Line

1. Ae as in Ami, Aedi (heel)
2. Aae as in Estimate, Aenak(Spectacle)
3. as in only, Om (prayer)
4. Au as in Autumn, Aurat (woman)
5. Nasal N -as in Uncle, Angoor (grape)
6. Aangh as in Aunt, Aankh(eye)
7. aei-rarely used

ए ऐ ओ औ अं ऑ अः..

The vowels are ae, aae, o, au, ungh, angh and aei (sanskrit) e.g. prataei -sanskrti for morning.

This completes the detached vowels

Vowel marks when used with consonants

First Line

1. Aa as in Master, Mama
2. little e as Miss, Mill (to meet)
3. Long ee as in Meat, Teer (Arrow)
4. oo as in Pull, Pashu (animal)
5. Long oo as in pool, Fool (flower).

The marks are Aa , i, ee, u , oo

Second Line

1. Ae as in made, Mez(table)
2. Aae as in Stack, Gas
3. as in Roe, Moti (pearl)
4. Au as in Crawley, Hathoda (hammer)
5. Ungh as in stung, Kanga (comb)
6. Angh as in Cant, Sanp (snake)
7. uggh (doubling) -no equivealent - as in Chh (six) rarely used.

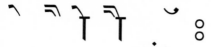

If you have stuck it out this far, well done!
As a test see if you can write down the English
words January, February ...December in Hindi
script and check it with the next Day. Also write
the numbers one, two .. till twenty as best as you
can.

Letter R

The letter R often has the short and long U placed
in the middle rather than at the bottom.
What are these words?

रुक   रूम

r-u-k (rook as in rookie)   r-oo-m (room)

A short diagonal stroke also gives an R sound
after a letter, usually placed below P or F. Note
the R here modifying the first word FAS to what?

फास ्फास

The answer is France! Note the nasal N dot over
the F.

A short sign like the one above the letter six on your keyboard is often put under the T give a Tr sound. What is this word?

$$\wedge \quad टक \; ट्रक$$

Yes, the R modifies the TK to give Truck. Another is the Ri sound put under M and N but also other letters. What is this word - (Hindi for dance)?

$$_c \quad नृतय$$

Answer is Nritya.

An R sound can also be placed ABOVE a letter where it is sounded BEFORE the letter it is placed. As a test see if you can read the word below.

$$^\cap \quad मार्क$$

DAY 14

Compare your writing in Hindi with the following. Do not worry if you get the 'spelling' slightly wrong. You may pronounce the months differently! It can be very hard to know when to put in the half letters. Give yourself five marks for each correct month you identify.

मे मार्च जूलाई डिसैम्बर एत्रिल जून सपटैम्बर औकटूबर नवैम्बर जैनुअरी फैबरुअरी औगस्ट

The correct answers are May March July December April June September October November January February August.
Now identify the following English numbers in the correct order. Five marks for each.

शरी सैवन टेन अेट थरटीन नाईन वान इलैवन टू सिफ्सटीन फिफटीन फोर टवैल्व सैवन्टीन सिक्स फाईव फौरटीन एटीन टवैन्टी नाईनटीन

The correct answers are 3 7 10 8 13 9 1 11 2 16 15 4 12 17 6 5 14 18 20 and 19.

If you get them all correct well done! Note the different ways that the A in eighteen and A in April can be written. If you feel confident try to write down the common English first names for boys and girls in Hindi and we will check next week

DAY 15

The next figure contains common English names, followed by Muslim boys and one Muslim girls name and finally common Hindu names. See if you can get them all correctly.

श्र्डरियु माइवल टिम अेन्थनी

डेविड बौबि शीन रेढिं पीटर

ल्सा सैरा जोन रारवी

रमज़ान हाइदर फारा

चॉद ऋषि ज्ञान त्रिभुवन गोविन्दा

ऐन्डरियु माइक्ल टिम ऐन्थनी

डेविड बौबि शेन रैंढिं पीटर

लृसा सैरा जोन राखी

रमज़ान हाइदर फारा

चाँद ऋषि ज्ञान त्रिभुवन गोविन्द

The answers are Andrew, Michael, Tim, Anthony.
The next line has David, Bobby, Shane, Randy,
Peter.
The third one is Larrisa, Sara, Joan and Indian
girls name Rakhi.
The fourth has Ramzan, Hyder, Fara.
The last one has Chand, Rishi, Gyan, Tribhuvan,
Govinda.

Now lets look at some common phrases

दिस इज़ आइ हेव रन औफ मनि

बो टू द ऋषि गार्ड दैट वुमन

पलीज़

वाट आर यू डुइग दिस इवनिग

टाइरैक्ट मी टू द बैंक पलीज़

घ्वाट टाईम डज़ द टरेन लीव

Were you able to read them all? The correct answers are: This is; Guard that woman please; Bow to the Rishi; what (note since there is no w in Hindi most Indians tend to pronounce w as v) are you doing this? I have run out of money; what time does the train leave? Direct me to the bank. See if you can make a stab at writing the following in Hindi. Write the letters but put the top line across a word afterwards. The remaining Hindi Days will concentrate on some short stories written in English with Hindi script.

DAY 16

These are the sentences from the last Day.

I have pain in my stomach,
I need to see a doctor,
I am sorry I don't understand Hindi,
I live in Canada,
How do I get to a hotel?
I want to get off at the next stop,
Where is the nearest telephone?
My name is,
Are you married?
So you speak English!
What is your telephone number?
Are u free to go out tonight?
I want to marry you.
This is how they are written in Hindi.

आइ हैव अ पेन माई स्टॅमक ।

Aai   haaev   a   paen   maaee   stmk

आई नीड टु सी ए डोकटर ।

Aaee need   tu   see   ae   dactar

आई ऐम सौरी आई डोंट अंडरसटैंं

Aaee aaem saari aaee don't andrstn

हिन्दी ।

hindi

आई लिव इन कानदा ।

Aaee   liv   in   kanada

हाओ डू आद गैट टू अ

how   du   aaee   get   tu   a

होटैल

hotel.

See if you can match the following sentences
with the ones in the shown below. One of them
has Hindi names. This Day has nearly all the
alphabet letters at least once, so if on going
through it a second time you can get all the
sentences correct, well done!

   A. Oil in China

B. Only Mark, Gyan, Rishee, Akshay, Tren made it.

C. I have a pain in my stomach

D. I need to see a doctor at once.

E. Thank the French

F. Shant do it

G. Yes the colour brown and Khakhi go well together

H. Oops John you made a mistake.

आइ हैव अ पेन इन माई स्टॅमक

षैस द कलर बराऊन ऐड रवारवी

गो वैल टुगैदर।

थैक द प्रैंचं

उप्स जौन यू मेड ए मिसटेक।

शॉट डु इट।

आई नीड टु सी ए डोकटर ऐट

वांस।

औइल इन चाइना ।
ओनली मार्क ज्ञान ऋषी अक्षे त्रन
मेड इट ।

The answers are 1=C; 2=G;
3=E;4=H;5=F;6=D;7=A;8=B

Let us look in detail how these sentences are made up. Some of the words are written as they might sound. You may not agree with the vowels or the half letters the pronunciations of which depends on where in the world you come from.

आइ हैव अ पेन इन माई
Aai   haaev   a   paen   in   maaee

स्टॅमक
stmk

यैस   द   कलर   बराऊन   ऐड
Yaaees the   klr   braaoon   aaend

रवारवी

khakhi

गो वैल टुगैदर।

go vaaeel tugaather

थैक द प्रैंच

Thank the French

उप्स जौन यू मेड अे

Oops john yu made a

मिसटेक।

mistake

शॉट डु इट।

Shant du it

आई नीड टु सी ए डोकटर

Aai need tu see aa dactar

ऐट वांस।

aaet vonce

औंइल इन चाइना ।

Auil   **in**   **chainaa**

ओनली मार्क ज्ञान ऋषी

Onlee   **mark**   **gyaan**   **rishee**

अक्षे त्रन

akshay tren

मेड इट ।

made   **it**

Some notes on the above. In sentence one note the
accent mark which looks like a half moon. It
signifies the accent is on T and not on S.
In 2 the word well is spelt vael as there is no
equivalent to W. You might write it as uvell to get
closer to the sound. In 3 note the r mark
modifying the F in French. In 4 there is a half P.
In 6 the aaet is often written with only a single ae
mark on top. In 8 note the r in mark over the k
modifies M the previous letter. The Sh sound here
is the more chesty Shh as in Shun, different from
the Sh in no. shine.

DAY 17

These are the sentences from the last Day.
I have pain in my stomach, I need to see a doctor,
I am sorry I dont understand hindi, I live in
canada
Here are the sentences translated into Hindi. Note
Hindi masculine words usually end in A e.g.
MAMA (uncle) while female end in i e.g. MAMI
(aunt)

मेरे पेट मे दरद है

मुभे डोक्टर कि ज़रुरत है

माफ करना मै हिन्दी नहीं समजता.

मै कानदा मे रहता हुं

the anwsers

मेरे	पेट	मे	दरद	है
maerae	**paet**	**mae**	**drd**	**haae**
mine	**stomach**	**in**	**pain**	**is**

मुझे   डोक्टर   कि

mujhae   **dactar**   **ki**

I   **doctor**   **of**

ज़रुरत   है

zrurt   **haae**

need   **have**

माफ करना   मै   हिन्दी   नहीं

Maaf   **krnaa**   **maae**   **hindee**   **nheen**

Forgive   **do**   **I**   **hindi**   **don't**

समजता.

smjta

understand

मै   कानदा   मे   रहता

Maae   **kanada**   **mae**   **rhta**

I   **Canada**   **in**   **live**

हुं

hun

do

Where is the nearest telephone? My name is, Are you married? So you speak English!

णज़दीक टेलिफोन कहां है

ोरा नाम है

क्या आप शादिशुदा है

तो आप इन्गलिश बोलति है

Here are the answers explained

णज़दीक	टेलिफोन	कहां
nzdeek	**telefon**	**kahan**
near	**telephone**	**where**

है

haae

is

रेरा	नाम	है
maaeraa	naam	haae
my	name	is

क्या	आप	शादिशुदा
kya	aap	shaadashudaa
what	you	married

है
haae
is

तो	आप	इन्गलिश	बोलति है
to	app	English	bolti haaen
so	you	English	speak do

What is your telephone number? What are you doing tonight? I want to marry you.

आप का टेलिफोन नम्बर कया है

आप शाम को कया कर रहीं है

मै तुम से शादी करना चाहता हुँ

Here are the answers.

आप	का	टेलिफोन	नम्बर
Aap	kaa	telefhan	nmbr
You	's	telephone	number

कया	है
kya	haae
what	is

आप	शाम	को	कया	कर
aap	shaam	ko	kya	kr
You	evening	at	what	do

रहीं	है
rheen	haaen
ring	are

मै तुम से शादी करना

Maae tum sae shaadee krnaa
Me you of marry do

चाहता हुँ

chahta hoon
want is

Extras sounds

Hindi being one of the Indo -European group of languages, nearly all the letters sound the same as in English, There are however a few extra sounds and these can cause some difficulty. Lets look at four of them. The first is the letter TTH, the second one in the figure below.

ट ढ ड द

T TTH D DH

ठण्डी ठीक हठी

The 1st and 3rd sounds are identical to English being T as in Tom and D as in Drum. The

fourth DH is just D sounded from the chest.
Touching the tip of the tongue on the
prominent ridge of the hard palate makes the
first hard T in Tom - test it out on yourself.
The third, hard D as in Drum is made by
touching the tongue further back. TTH is
midway between the two, ie on the uppermost
ridge of the hard palate.

Were you able to read the words? Here are the
answers.

ठण्डी	ठीक	हठी
tthndee	**ttheek**	**htthee**
cold	**correct**	**stubborn**

It takes a little practice but is not difficult to
sound TTH correctly.

Next we have the AD'(ughD) sound . Touch
the tongue on top as in D, now roll it back
further and then unroll it without touching the
palate - this gives you the ughD' sound. In
Hindi this sound is marked by a dot below the
D and Dh sounds. Read the words below.

ड   ढ   ड़   ढ़

D   **DH**   **AD**   **ADH**

खड़ लड़ाई पढ़

The answers

खड़   लड़ाई   पढ

khad   **L ad'aae**   **padh**

stand   **fight**   **read**

Another in the T series is the soft t.. If you make the T sound with the tongue and then the THE sound touching the tongue to the top of the upper teeth then the soft t is in-between this and the TH as in THanks. So here the tip of tongue touches the bottom of the upper teeth and the first third of the tongue is pressed against the teeth and the palate. Read the following words.

त भूत तेल तुम

and the answers

त भूत तेल तुम

T   **bhoot**   **t'ael**   **t'um**

         Ghost   **oil**   **you**

The tongue touches the front of the palate for the CH as in CHina sound. For the CHH sound the tongue touches the palate slightly more back.

छ   छलांग छत

The answers

छ   छलांग   छत

Chh   **chhlaang**   **cht'**

           Jump   **root**

You can often find out from the local temple about any Hindi teachers to get these correct. As these are the letters, which often-non-Hindi speakers tend to mispronounce, it is worth making an effort to get them right.

In the next Day, we will build up a vocabulary of the common words.

DAY 18

How to write Hindi letters
A step means you take the pen off the paper. Most
Hindi letters can be written in 2 or 3 steps. The
last step is the drawing of the horizontal line at the
top. Experienced Hindi writers can reduce them
further by for example retracing their pen back up
a vertical stem.

This and the next Day cover almost all the
compound letters, vowels etc. so we can
familiarize ourselves with all the letters and are
able to read them when we scan in a few stories
from publications. Some of the steps in writing
certain letters are left for you to do as an exercise.
Note the faint arrow line, the tail of the arrow
gives you the direction from which the pen starts.
The next figure contains the first two lines of the
alphabet. The first five letters are the Gutturals all
produced from the back of the throat and the next
five from CH onwards - the palatals-so called
because the tongue strikes the hard palate.
Note that a very few Hindi letters can be written
in more than one way. JH and A and AA are the
best examples. Compare JH with that in Day 13

Gutturals
GUTTURALS

क K | ↓ १ | क | क
Step 1 | Step 2 | Step 3 | 3

ख KH | २ | २। | ख | ख
Step 1 | Step 2 | Step 3 | Step 4 | 4

ग G | ↑ | ग। | ग | 3

घ GH | ट | ध | घ | 2 or 3

ड़ N | ड | ड | ड़ | 3

PALATALS

च CH | च | च | Steps 2

छ CHH | छ | छ | छ | 3 Steps

ज J-2 | भ | भ | झ JH-3

ञ N-3 | ० | ञ | ञ

Next is the cerebrals because the tongue points up to the head, the dentals where the tongue strikes the upper teeth and the labials where the lips are closed. It is worth getting a pen and writing each on a piece of paper as you read the next figure.

Cerebrals

ट   ठ   ठ   ड   ढ ड   ढ ण ण

T-2   TTH-2   D-2   DH-2   aD-3   aDH-3   N-3

Dentals

त त थ द ध ध न न

     T-2   TH-2   THE-2   THHE-2   N-2

Labials

प प ५ फ फ व ब ब भ भ म

     P-2   F-3   B-3   BH-2   M-2

Now follow the semi vowels, the sibilants or s sound and finally H the aspirant.

SEMI VOWELS

य र ल ल व
Y-2   R-2   L-2   V-2

SIBILANTS

श शा श प प ष
SH-3   SHH-3

ASPIRANT

ङ ह ह
H-3

Here is how the vowels are written. Ugh is formed in three steps. AA in four by adding an aa mark to ugh.

उ अ अ आ इ इ ई

ugh-3 aa-4 i-2 ee-3

उ उ उ ऊ ऊ अं अँ

u-2 00-3 ughn-4 aan-5

ऽ ऽ ए ऐ ओ ओ औ

ae-3 aae-4 o-5(from aa) au-6(from o)

Aan of course if formed from Ugh etc. In the top part of the figure below are the vowel marks. Note little i is actually added after the letter e.g. M is written down first as in the English word miss below; when it appears before the letter M.

| accent | aa-2 | i-3 | ee-3 | u-1 | oo-1 |

| 'n-1 | aan-2 | ae-1 | aae-2 | aee -2 | r-1 | r-1 | r-1 | ri-1 |

म मि मिस म मे मै मैप

miss   map

माक मार्क म मृ मूग

mark   mrig (deer)

प प्रात:

praataee (sanskrit-morning)

Note the mark for r which follow the letter in the word Prate and the ri which modifies M in Mrig. But that the top r modifies the previous letter e.g.

in the word Mark where it modifies the preceding letter M even though it put over the K. Finally note the two vertical dots which give an ae sound and mostly used in Sanskrit words eg in the word Prataee as above built up from P then adding a r mark in the foot of the P etc. Prate Kal in Sanskrit means morning.

Next, we look at compound letters. There are about 10 of these although only KSH, TR ,GY, SHR , and Ri are considered as part of the alphabet . These are written by starting with the vertical line first.

The next figure has Z, N, Ru, ROO, Hy, Hm, LRi, and the symbol for peace OM

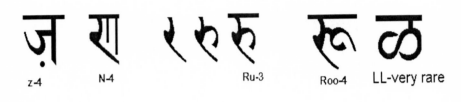

z-4   N-4   Ru-3   Roo-4   LL-very rare

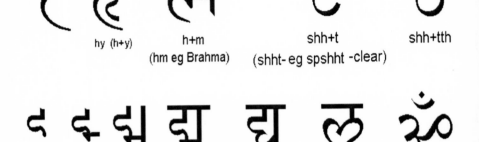

hy (h+y)   h+m   shh+t   shh+tth
           (hm eg Brahma)   (shht- eg spshht -clear)

d+m (dm)   d+y(dy eg vidya)   Lri   OM-(Peace)-4

The following figure contains some interesting letters. On the top line is the guttural form of N combined with K, and next to it g. Sometimes ugh and AA are written as in this figure. Again, it is important to know these so that one may is not surprised when reading a magazine.

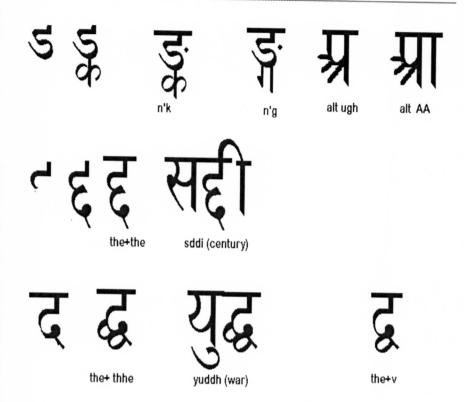

ड ड़
n'k

ड़ ड़ं
n'g

ड़
alt ugh

ग्र ग्रा
alt AA

 द्ध द्ध द्ध
the+the

सद्दी
sddi (century)

द द्ध
the+ thhe

युद्ध
yuddh (war)

द्व
the+v

THE can also be combined with a couple of letters. One of them as in the figure above gives the word for war -yudh.

Lets have a look in this Day at some doubled letters. These below are the common letters and a couple of examples are given.

ठ्ठ
tth+tth

ट्ट
t+t   eg lattu
(top toy)

लट्टू

ड्ड
d+d

त + त = त्त
t'+t'   t't'   eg.

कुत्ता
kut't'aa -dog

न + न = न्न
n+n   nn   eg.

अन्न
ughnn -grain

Finally, lets check we remember all the half letters. Although this Day may seem difficult, you have met nearly all the letters before. Some like the t and d's are just smaller version of the full letter while jh and r do not seem to have any half letter form

क ख ग घ ङ   च छ ज ञ
k   kh g gh n   ch chh j   n

ट ठ ड ढ ण   त थ द न
t   tth d ddh n   t'   th theh n

प फ ब भ म य ल व श स
p   f   b   bh m   y   L   v   sh s

DAY 19

Next, let us look at compound letters. There are about 10 of these although only KSH , TR ,GY, SHR , and Ri are considered as part of the alphabet. These are written by starting with the vertical line first.

The next figure has Z, N, Ru, ROO, Hy, Hm, LRi, and the symbol for peace OM

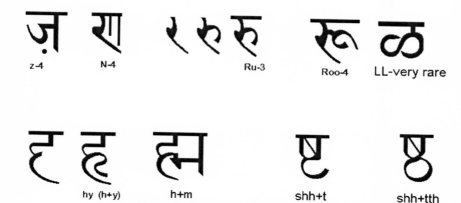

z-4   N-4   Ru-3   Roo-4   LL-very rare

hy (h+y)   h+m   shh+t   shh+tth
            (hm eg Brahma)   (shht- eg spshht -clear)

d+m (dm)   d+y(dy eg vidya)   Lri   OM-(Peace)-4

The following figure contains some interesting letters. On the top line is the guttural form of N combined with K, and next to it g.
Sometimes ugh and AA are written as in this figure. Again, it is important to know these so that you are not surprised when reading a magazine.

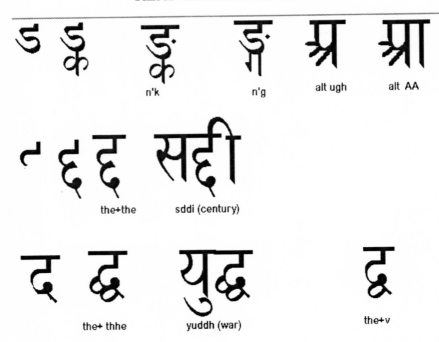

ड ड़ ड़ू ङ ञ्र ञ्रा

n'k   n'g   alt ugh   alt AA

ः ६ द्द सद्दी

the+the   sddi (century)

द द्व युद्ध द्व

the+ thhe   yuddh (war)   the+v

THE can also be combined with a couple of letters. One of them as in the figure above gives the word for war -yudh.

Lets have a look in this rather long Day at some doubled letters. These below are the common and a couple of examples are given.

Finally, lets check that we remember all the half letters. Although this Day may seem difficult, you have seen nearly all the letters before. Some like the t and d's are just smaller version of the full letter while jh and r do not seem to have any half letter form

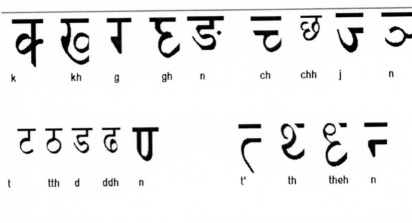

क	ख	ग	घ	ङ	च	छ	ज	ञ
k	kh	g	gh	n	ch	chh	j	n

ट	ठ	ड	ढ	ण	त	थ	ध	न
t	tth	d	ddh	n	t'	th	theh	n

प	फ	ब	भ	म	य	र	ल	व	श	स
p	f	b	bh	m	y	L	v	sh	s

Read the following sentences in the next figures . You wont meet any harder than these and if you can read them correctly you can consider yourself as having mastered the Hindi alphabet.

बुद्धिमान पुरूष को ज्ञान बहुत है .

ब्रह्मापुत्रा , कृष्णा , नर्मदा नदिया हैं .

Answers are

बुद्धिमान पुरूष को ज्ञान बहुत है .

B-u-THETHE-i-M-aa-N	P-u-R-oo-SHH	K-o	GY-aa-N	B-H-u-T'	H-aae
Wise	Man	of	knowledge	lot	has

ब्रह्मापुत्रा , कृष्णा , नर्मदा नदिया हैं .

B-r-HM-aa-P-u-T-r-aa	K-r-shh-N-aa	N-r-M-THE-aa	N-THE-i-Y-aa	H-aae-n
Brahmaputra	Krishna	Naramada	rivers	are

In this figure, there are more compound letters.

¹ विद्यार्थि पड़ रहा है .

² पद्मा नदि पर्वत से आती है .

³ हिन्दी, उर्दू राष्ट्र की भाषाएँ हैं .

Note in sentence 1 below in the first word vidhyarthi, the little i is written before the v but pronounced after it. In contrast the r mark is written over the TH but pronounced after the DY

1 विद्यार्थि पड़ रहा है.

ViDYarTHi   PD'   RHaa   Haae

Student   reading   doing   is

2 पद्मा नदि पर्वत से आती है.

PDMaa   NDi   PrVT'   Sae   AAT'EE   Haae

Padma   river   mountain   from   comes   does

3 हिन्दी, उर्दू राष्ट्र की भाषाएं है.

HiND'ee   UrDoo   RaaSHTr   Kee   BHaaSHHaaAEn'   Haaen

Hindi   Urdu   Country   of   languages   are

DAY 20

Vocabulary

We will look at some common words in Hindi. Its not possible to put the whole dictionary here so only the most common ones are being shown.

In Western India Urdu words are more common while in Eastern India the more sanskrit type predominate. In some cases both are given. Most people in India understand English so its not absolutely vital to know Hindi to get around.

Each set of new letters is put on a new line so you can follow them more easily. The pronunciation guide is given below.

I, You (respectful), You (familiar), He She It They, Mine, Yours

His, Hers, Its, Ours, Theirs, Why, What, Where, When, How, Who, Yes, No, Maybe, Father (Hindi), Father (Urdu), Wife(Hindi), Wife(U), Husband.

मै आप तुम वह मेरा तुम्हारा

उसका हमारा उनहोंका क्यों कया

कहाँ कब कैसे किसने हाँ नही

शायद पिता बाप स्त्री बीवि पति

The words in Hindi are:

maaen, aap, t'um, vh, maera, t'umhaaraa
uskaa, hmaaraa, unhonkaa, kyon, kyaa
khaan, kb, kaaesae, kisnae, haan, nahin
shaayd, pit'aa,baap, stri or pt'ni, beevi, pt'i
Let us have a look at some animals.
animal (h), animal(u), elephant, camel, horse
lion (u) tiger, tigress, lion(h), leopard
bear (h), bear(u), crocodile, monkey
rabbit, goat, sheep, tortoise, pig
mouse, fish , deer, donkey , snake

पशु जानवर हाथी ऊँट घोड़ा
बबर शेर शेर शेरनि सिंह चीता
भालू रीछ मगरमच्छ बंदर
खरगोश बकरी भेड़ कछुआ सूर
चुहा मछली हिरण गधा साँप

Printed in the United States
69162LVS00002B/20